JOHN CARSON LESTER JR

The MLM Screen Pass Tactic

PureHeartsInternational.com
Do Well By Doing Good

First edition

This book was professionally typeset on Reedsy.
Find out more at reedsy.com

For the "little guy" and "little gal" in the network marketing industry, people I understand and still relate to today despite my decades of substantial achievement in the industry.

"People are not interested in your product or your business; they are interested in solving their own problems." -John Carson Lester Jr

Contents

Foreword

"John Lester's Pied Piper Principles are good. I have known John since the early days of Internet Marketing. In fact, he helped me fight off MLM scam artists on the old AOL MLM Forums. I've subscribed to his newsgroup for years and respect John's marketing wisdom highly. In fact, I have beat him about the head and shoulders to print it in Book format. In fact, I took his CDs and sent the MP3 files to my transcriptionist and am pushing him to get it edited now. WHY? Because it needs to be kept on hand every day as a quick reference on "How To Do Internet Marketing" or any Marketing for that matter. When he gets the book done it will be one of the few books that I sell on my MLM Consumer Protection website." -Rod Cook aka The MLM WatchDog

Preface

I don't just think, I *know* that every "little guy" and "little gal" in the network marketing industry failing over and over again and jumping from one MLM program to another over and over again ad nauseaum to their own great frustration and oftentimes destruction would be able to create success for themselves in any MLM they do as soon as they thoroughly read, comprehended and incorporated the rock-solid and time-proven principles and skills found in my 4 MLM works in this exact order: 1) THE BEST OF THE BEST; 2) PIED PIPER PRINCIPLES; 3) the MLM SCREEN PASS TACTIC; 4) the SELF-EMPLOYMENT 101 SERIES; and finally 5) the MLM IGNORANCE TRAP.

Writing from Bacolod City, Negros Occidental in the Philippines on November 22, 2018, John Carson Lester Jr, Owner of MyForbiddenLeads.com

Acknowledgement

As always, I'm both deeply inspired and indebted by the love and for the support I've received in the writing of the MLM SCREEN PASS TACTIC by the three special women in my life; my fiance Lynlyn Balberde, my sister Jennifer Ann Lester and my mother Armina Virginia Lester; and my late dad, John Carson Lester Sr.

1

Introduction

Hi, Friend. John Carson Lester Jr here. You know, your friendly neighborhood Mentor to the Online Marketing Gurus who in the mid-1990s taught the likes of Jonathan Mizel and Marlon Sanders how to online market (click your "Testimonials - ALL" link at MyForbiddenLeads.com). Your one of only three IRS-registered Founding Members of your Distributor Rights Association. Your DRA Executive Director of Communications. Your DRA Executive Director of Media and Publicity. Owner of the world's only full service MLM genealogy lead list service bureau and full service marketing consulting firm. Your owner of the world's largest full service bulk email company focusing on MLM genealogy lead lists since 1996. Your publisher of not only your MLM SCREEN PASS TACTIC, but also your THE BEST OF THE BEST, your PIED PIPER PRINCPLES, your SELF EMPLOYMENT 101 SERIES and your MLM IGNORANCE TRAP Amazon Kindle eBooks and Amazon Paperback books. Your May 2005 New Kid on the Block Network Marketing Business Journal Company. Featured in WIRED. Your $80,000+ in a single month earner. Your transactor w/over 100,000+ people in over 100+ countries around the world. Your 947+ pages of testimonials generator. Your gentleman and a scholar...yatta, yatta, yatta, etc. :)

2

Minimum Pre-Requisites

In order for you to get your maximum benefit out of your MLM Screen Pass Tactic purchase, we're assuming that you already have the minimum pre-requisite of deeply understanding that recruiting friends, family and opportunity seekers is the path to your own MLM destruction and that only recruiting real network marketers is the path to your own MLM success. For the necessary background info on this topic, simply click on your appropriate FAQs links near the very top of http://www.MyForbiddenLeads.com and read and learn.

3

The Solution

And how do I, John Carson Lester Jr, know all of this, you might ask?

Because I, John Carson Lester Jr, starting back in 1992, was recruiting other MLMers from the old pre-Internet commercial online service MLM message boards on Prodigy, CompuServe and America Online (especially on AOL where, at its zenith in the mid-1990s, I'd estimate that perhaps as many as a half million or more MLMers gathered in that one place) a full decade before most people even got on the Internet. Just ask Rod Cook who was a frequent poster on my personally-owned world's-largest-at-the-time opt-in global email discussion list on the topic of online marketing:

"John Lester's Pied Piper Principles are good. I have known John since the early days of Internet Marketing. In fact, he helped me fight off MLM scam artists on the old AOL MLM Forums. I've subscribed to his newsgroup for years and respect John's marketing wisdom highly. In fact, I have beat him about the head and shoulders to print it in Book format. In fact, I took his CDs and sent the MP3 files to my transcriptionist and am pushing him to get it edited now. WHY? Because it needs to be kept on hand every day as a quick reference on "How To Do Internet Marketing" or any Marketing for that matter. When he gets the book done it will be one of the few books that I sell on my MLM Consumer Protection website." -Rod Cook aka The MLM WatchDog

See, Friend, when I began prospecting other MLMers to join my MLM way back in 1992, I quickly discovered something very "shocking." And that was the fact that most MLMers simply weren't interested in joining my MLM. In fact, most MLMers, I discovered, were already in a MLM that they wanted ME to join THEM in right there and then! And why is that? The answer is because people are naturally selfish and self-centered. And because people are naturally selfish and self-centered, we, as wise and mature and successful businesspersons, must approach the marketplace unselfishly. To illustrate people's natural selfishness and self- centeredness and how to overcome this and how to turn their selfishness in to our own advantage and profit, the next two to three pages are taken directly from points 17 and 18 of my TBOTB series (The Best of the Best):

17) We understand that we CANNOT be FOCUSED on OUR NEEDS, OUR SURVIVAL, the $ that WE NEED to make it, pay the rent, buy groceries, etc, etc, etc.

We understand that we HAVE to be FOCUSED on our PROSPECT's NEEDS and the WAY for THAT to happen is to HAVE A CAUSE BIGGER THAN OURSELVES!

We understand that the only way to keep ourselves motivated in the long term is to have a HIGHER PURPOSE than just our own selfish needs.

As soon as we do the above, along with stopping worrying about whether we "make a sale" or not for OURSELVES, and START focusing on HELPING to create another SUCCESS STORY out of your prospect's life or business, THAT is when we will start ENJOYING SUCCESS!

SUCCESS...it's an INSIDE job. That's where it all starts and ends!

And, of course, we understand that when the "sale" is made ("yes" DECISION), the REAL SALE has JUST BEGUN.<g>

So don't get excited about SALES, consider yourself an AMBAS-SADOR of your products and services looking to benefit a new country that you want to establish excellent diplomatic relations with (your prospect) and you'll be JUST FINE no matter what any SINGLE individual SAYS, good, bad, or indifferent.

And by being a hard working, industrious AMBASSADOR that has created for himself/herself SO MANY opportunities to establish relations with SO MANY countries, you'll NEVER put pressure on any single country to establish relations, and thereby, paradoxically, end up having MANY MORE nations *want* to establish relations with YOU as a result.

18) We understand that if we come off sounding like a salesperson, we lose.

EVERYONE in life is FIGHTING THE WAR of life!

If you come off sounding like someone who is going to HELP THEM FIGHT *THEIR* WARS (and everybody's *wars* are *different* although there are many similar *battles*), then you will win the highest percentage of the time that you could possibly win.

Which is the best that you could possibly do, which is what you want.

Why is that? Why is this approach the best way to get people COMMUNICATING WITH YOU?

Well, think of the following picture that hangs in sales offices across the nation! BACKGROUND: medieval war, soldiers on two opposing sides fighting on horses, using swords, bows and arrows, and other primitive weapons. FOREGROUND: tent, with a salesperson on one side, arms crossed, legs crossed, looking very cocky and confident, standing next to a machine gun! On the other side of the tent is a General whose gaze is fixed on the war proceeding on the battlefield, and a Junior Officer trying to get the General's attention by stating, "General, there is a salesperson here to see you!" The General cannot see the salesperson because the salesperson is out of sight on the other side of the tent, and besides, his gaze is fixed on the battlefield, and he replies to the Junior Officer, irritably, "I don't have any time to see a SALESPERSON! Can't you see that I am fighting a WAR here!"

Most of you fail in your marketing efforts because your MES-

SAGE (the Junior Officer), is WRONG! You broadcast, in so many ways, rather, you EMOTIONALLY PROJECT, THAT YOU ARE JUST TRYING to SELL SOMETHING to the other person!

Guess what?!

The OTHER PERSON doesn't want to buy your stuff!

Why? Because s/he is SO CONSUMED, SO DISTRACTED, STRUGGLING trying to WIN THEIR WARS OF LIFE, that if you approach them sounding like a SALESPERSON, they are not going to remove their eyes from their BATTLEFIELD and they will NEVER *see* your MACHINE GUN (MyForbiddenLeads.com)!

You're *just* a DISTRACTION! of their attention! from THEIR WAR! if you're viewed as "just" being a salesperson!

THEY DON'T WANT TO BUY YOUR STUFF! BUT THEY *DO* WANT TO WIN THEIR WAR! SO YOUR JOB IS TO GET THEIR ATTENTION AND THE WAY YOU GET THEIR ATTENTION IS TO FOCUS THEIR FOCUS ON THE FACT THAT YOU'RE THERE TO HELP THEM WIN THEIR WAR!

Now, wouldn't things have been different IF, INSTEAD of telling the Junior Officer that a SALESPERSON was here to see the General, that salesperson told the Junior Officer (the messenger) that there was a person to see the General that had a piece of war equipment that would VANQUISH the entire army of the enemy in mere seconds?!

Do you think that MESSAGE would have GOT THE GENERAL'S

ATTENTION?!

You bet it would!

The POWER OF WORDS can never be underestimated in the world of sales/marketing!

LITTLE THINGS make ALL THE DIFFERENCE IN THE WORLD!

You need to IMMEDIATELY, at the BEGINNING of the contact, come off sounding like you are interested in helping this person FIGHT THEIR WAR! NOT YOURS! (The End of points 17 and 18 from John Lester's TBOTB or The Best of The Best).

4

More Details

Now, you may be wondering, what does points 17 and 18 from John Lester's "The Best of the Best" (TBOTB) have to do with overcoming the "competitive threat" or "resistance" or "reverse pitch" problem that is at the heart of what your MLM Screen Pass Tactic is all about here? Answer: everything!

See, Friend, just like we describe in great detail on your 5 hour 50 minute PiedPiperPrinciple CD/eBook/Paperback, a high percentage of prospects from any given MLM genealogy list, when you first approach them, are currently in a multi-level marketing program and experiencing what we call their "honeymoon" period. Now, it very well may be their 838th "marriage" to a new network marketing company, and they may have been on 837 honeymoons before, but somehow, inexplicably and without any logical rationale, you can rest assured that they are absolutely certain that they have finally found "the one" with whom they are going to spend the rest of their life!

Now, just close your eyes for a moment and think back to a time when you felt the most passion for some significant other in your life...and then think how you would have felt towards anyone that would have had the audacity and the downright obscene rudeness to suddenly pop up out of nowhere and even suggest (much less dare to even apply pressure) that you leave your significant other for someone else that you knew absolutely nothing about anyways?!

If you're like most women, you'd probably want to claw their eyes out! And if you're like most men, you'd probably want to punch their lights out!

Well, guess what, friend, that's exactly how that other MLMer feels when you come along pitching your MLM and trying to take them away from their MLM (spouse) while on their honeymoon no less! They want to claw your eyes out/punch your lights out!

Not exactly the way to "win friends and influence people" now, is it?!

So what's the solution, you may ask?

Well, after getting no where for awhile in my online prospecting efforts on the AOL MLM message boards way back in 1992, Friend, I asked my self that very same question!

Fortunately for me, however, I had a previous sales career experience from which to draw upon for answers. See, Friend, coming fresh out of college, in 1985, my first serious career job was as a life insurance agent for the 3rd largest life insurance company in the USA, The Equitable.

I had just finished telemarketing my way thru college including a stint my senior year setting appointments for a State Farm agent and so I hit the phones with real gusto to launch my promising new post-college Equitable Life sales career.

Wham. Reality hit. Guess what?

I discovered that, unlike my senior year part-time telemarketing job for State Farm where I was offering savings on homeowner and automobile policies, cold-call prospecting people for life in-surance policy sales was an entirely different league altogether.

Why?

Well, near as I could figure out, people just weren't all that excited about talking about their own impending death!

Who woulda thunk it?!

So I said to myself, "Self, we've got to come up with a workaround here. Just like the old-time door to door salesmen have done down thru the ages, I've got to find a better way to 'get my foot in to the prospect's door' and this approach of leading with 'talking about death' just isn't getting the job done!"

So guess what I did, Friend?

I went and got my investment licenses that permitted me to

sell mutual funds, real estate limited partnerships and even stocks and bonds! Then I immediately changed my telephone prospecting pitch from telling people that I wanted to stop by and talk to them about death and dying to a telephone prospecting pitch where I told people that I wanted to stop by to talk to them about improving their financial future in the here and the now while they were still alive and able to enjoy it!

Think my empty appointment book started filling up, Friend? Yes, and HOW! The improvement was both immediate and dramatic!

5

But Don't Bait And Switch!

And so now you might think that I went to the homes of all of these new prospects and "baited and switched them" from talking about investments into actually selling the life insurance and "cleaned up," right?!

Wrong!

See, remember, Friend, the "secret" to getting rich is that the rich get rich (at least the honest rich) by unselfishly helping people to solve their problems and to win their wars (of life as described in TBOTB point 18 earlier)!

And I practiced that "secret" by NEVER attempting to sell life insurance to those people who graciously opened up their homes to me to talk about investments. After I left their homes, I have no doubt that there were many married couples who looked down at my life insurance business card in their hands and then up at each other in amazement when it dawned on them that, for the first time in their lives, a life insurance agent had walked in to their home and never even talked, not even for a moment, about life insurance (unless they brought it up first)!

See, Friend, real selling is all about TRUST! People only buy from those people and those companies in whom they TRUST! And I knew that already from years of running my own businesses as a kid of various kinds ranging from lemonade stands in my parent's front yard to my own large paper route in my neighborhood for several years in middle school to my own large Fuller Brush sales route territory in my entire city in high school.

Now, Friend, life insurance companies were designed to pay agents large commissions for selling life insurance. Not for selling investments. We didn't make a whole lot of commission selling investments as life insurance agents.

And so you have no idea how many of those nights for the first six months or so I walked out of people's homes with a $100 per month IRA mutual fund investment where I had just earned a net whopping 73 cents or something like that.

But far more important than the 73 cents, as I knew from years of previous entrepreneurial experience, was the value of having obtained yet another TRUSTING CUSTOMER. And, as time went on over the next few weeks and months, what do you think happened? Those trusting customers started asking ME about life insurance! And so what do you think I did! I SOLD it to them (actually, they BOUGHT IT from me)!

6

The Problem

You most likely purchased your MLM Screen Pass Tactic because you purchased a MLM genealogy lead list and, despite assurances to the contrary by various false gurus, quickly discovered that it wasn't an easy glide path to MLM fame and fortune.

And why was that? Was it because you're not a very good telemarketer/salesperson? As a person who telemarketed his way thru college, frankly, that might be a small part of it. That is, if you happen to not be very good on the phone.

But, Friend, truth be known, prospecting MLM genealogy lists is a very difficult task for even the most talented and experienced of telemarketers/salespeople/MLMers. At least it is at the very beginning. Even for the Great Ones.

Why is that, you might ask?

Well, it's very simple. It's due to what I call the "competitive threat" or "resistance" or "reverse pitch" problem. More on this problem and its solution below.

7

Learning How And When To Take Their Temperature

And so I began to "take their temperature" from just talking to them and asking questions whereby I developed a sixth sense and a feel and learned the "signs and the signals" that indicated to me when it was the right time LATER in the RELATIONSHIP to talk about life insurance.

As a result, after six months of selling a whole lot of small commission investment accounts but not selling much life insurance, I went back and sold life insurance to a high percentage of these many, many, MANY investment account customers that I had patiently cultivated. And you guessed it! My life insurance sales over the next year went ABSOLUTELY THRU THE ROOF!

And, as a result, The Equitable offered me only the second corporate license ever offered to an agent at my 3rd largest Equitable agency where I worked. The first fellow was 20+ years my senior, had an MBA, and was pulling down about $5 million dollars per year in commissions with a very large support staff!

That's what the corporate license did for you. By paying you more than twice the regular commission scale, it allowed you to take the surplus commissions and hire a support staff to help leverage your business. By that time it was late 1986 (I had graduated in May of 1985) and I turned down this amazing Equitable offer to instead accept a competing offer to work as a full-fledged stock, bond and commodities broker for Prudential-Bache Securities (the stock bond and commodities firm that the Prudential had bought a few years earlier). I worked at Bache and in the securities industry until 1992 when I began transitioning myself into self-employment and the network marketing industry.

8

STPBTBED (See Twenty People Belly To Belly Every Day)!

(Note: 1997 email written by John Carson Lester continues from the end of Chapter 8): You need to have 20 pennies by your computer every day. You have to start off with something like this: 1000 contacts a day to get 187 hits on your autoresponder per day, then turn around and contact ALL 1000 again asking them about their opportunities and remind them that you emailed them the other day, you get about 50 or so people now emailing you back and forth and you ASK THEM QUESTIONS about their businesses so you can find out what their NEEDS and WANTS are, and when you KNOW a REASONABLE AMOUNT about their business, tell them if they do A (order), you'll GET THEM B, C, D, etc (and customize those emotionally-laden benefit statements to BEST PUSH their hot buttons AS they REVEALED THEM TO YOU), and you

KEEP FILLING UP THE PIPELINE WITH NEW CONTACTS

so that you are CONSTANTLY DOING THIS WITH

NEW PEOPLE

so that you can be ABCing (Always Be Closing), so that you CONSTANTLY

have AT LEAST 20 people a day

that you HAVE PROPERLY WORKED INTO THE RIGHT POSITION (according to the directions above), where you are JUSTIFIED and asking at THE RIGHT TIME the CLOSING QUESTION more or less in the manner that I indicated above, and by getting

20 DECISIONS a day,

you'll end up getting 1-2 or sometimes more sales per day. The rest will be noes. But you will be PAID EXACTLY THE SAME FOR A YES AS A NO since you KNOW that you get paid for getting DECISIONS asked at the right point of the sales process and that the HIGHEST PAID PERSON is the person that gets the MOST DECISIONS (most of which will always be no).

Put 20 pennies by your computer every day and do not stop putting out teasers until at the end of the day you can honestly be able to move those 20 pennies to the other side of the computer after working them to the right point in the sales process and asking those 20 people the CLOSING QUESTION.

Secret of ALL SALES SUCCESS as given to me by my first sales manager:

STPBTBED.

See twenty people

BELLY TO BELLY

every day.

Let me tell you how you get "BELLY TO BELLY" in cyberspace.

You ASK QUESTIONS. And you would be amazed at how more quickly most people will SPILL THEIR GUTS TO YOU in the PRIVACY and ANONYMITY of cyberspace. MORE than what they will usually do FACE TO FACE!

BELLY TO BELLY means filling up the pipeline so consistently with NEW PEOPLE that every day you have 20 people worked to the right place in the sales process as described above so that you can be asking the CLOSING QUESTION of 20 people to get, on average, probably about 18 noes and 2 yeses.

Folks, the above, on top of SINALOA (safety in numbers, law of averages), filling up the PIPELINE (what we do today doesn't show up until tomorrow; what we do this week doesn't show up until next week; what we do this month...next month; this quarter...next quarter; this year...next year; this decade...next decade; this life...next life), and the principle of CONSISTENCY thru the application of your DMO (Daily Method of Operation) to CREATE MOMENTUM (people-momentum-volume-checks), are pretty much

ALL THE HALLOWED, TIME-HONORED SECRETS of

sales/marketing.

FYI!!

Keep up the GREAT WORK, EVERYBODY!<g>

[:-)

John Carson Lester Jr, Creator of the gemSTARS-R-NICErs SYSTEMS!

"One's success in LIFE, much less any SINGLE endeavour, is DIRECTLY PROPORTIONAL to the amount of FRUSTRATION that one has successfully encountered, successfully endured and successfully overcome! This is why all entrepreneurial success DEPENDS on a SUFFICIENT number of 'failures.'" Original Quote from John Lester, November, 1996

End of 1997 email.

9

Even More Details

But what does this life insurance selling story have to do with your "competitive threat" or "resistance" or "reverse pitch" problem when prospecting MLM genealogy lists, you may ask? Answer: everything! See, friend, when I first started prospecting other MLMers on the old AOL message boards and first began encountering the "competitive threat" and "resistance" and "reverse pitches" problem from these other MLMers absolutely in love with their mlm (and not mine), it instantly reminded me very much of the same dilemma that I faced when I discovered that prospecting people about their impending death for life insurance sales also wasn't a very popular nor effective thing to do.

So, I said to myself, "Self, you developed an effective workaround when you encountered resistance to getting life insurance appointments and selling life insurance. You're just going to have to develop an effective workaround now that you've encountered 'competitive threat' reverse-pitch resistance to selling MLM opportunities to other MLMers!"

And, guess what, Friend, I did just exactly that very thing!

I developed your MLM Screen Pass Tactic!

Now, before I delineate your MLM Screen Pass Tactic, it's important for you to understand what a Screen Pass is. For those of you that follow American style football (with the oval ball, not the round ball that Americans call soccer), you immediately recognize the Screen Pass as being a play in the football playbook. Wikipedia defines a Screen Pass as...

...a type of "trick play" in American football much like a draw. During a screen pass, many things are going on at the same time in order to fool the defense into thinking a long pass is being thrown, when in fact the pass is merely a short one, just beyond the defensive linemen. Screens are usually deployed against aggressive defenses that rush the passer. Because screens invite the defense to rush the quarterback, it leaves fewer defenders behind the rushers to stop the play.

Now that you know what a Screen Pass is in American football, Friend, you need to know what a MLM Screen Pass is. And to learn what a MLM Screen Pass is you're going to want to read and study the following year 1997 email written by John Carson Lester Jr. But before you read the following year 1997 email, you want to understand the context in which it was written. See the domain below of discussion-lists.com? John Carson Lester Jr is the person who originally created and registered that domain name. I later, in 1999, sold discussion-lists.com for $500 to Chris of Sparknet.net when I no longer had any need for that domain. But, at that time, discussion-lists.com was the home

25

of the world's largest Bulk Email University, for lack of a better term.

Who was on that list that I, John Carson Lester Jr, both owned and led? Jonathan Mizel. Marlon Sanders. Rod Cook. And every other big name marketer that you recognize today but who were little known or at least far less known way back in 1997. Why were they and over 4,000 (that was a HUGE opt-in unmoderated DISCUSSION list back in those days, especially for MLM) other aspiring online marketers on this list?

Because they had bought a very special software program that I created and owned called NICErsPRO (one of John Carson Lester Jr's personally owned corporations is called NICErsPRO-MOTIONS, Inc). NICErsPRO is known today as MyForbidden-Leads.com. About 1,000+ of the 4,000+ NICErsPRO customers were also my affiliates for selling said $400 NICErsPRO software (including Jonathan Mizel). And they religiously read and/or participated in this global email discussion list because this list taught them, under John Carson Lester Jr's leadership and tutelage, more about marketing and online marketing and online network marketing than any single source had ever taught them before. That's why you see testimonials from Rod Cook and Jonathan Mizel and Marlon Sanders in your "Testimonials - ALL" link at MyForbiddenLeads.com.

Mizel's testimonial came from an email he wrote me and Sander's testimonial came from a public post that he posted over gemstars-r-nicers@discussion-lists.com. Today the following 1997 email is merely one of 1100+ "Best of the Best" training web pages (now assigned to March 5th of every year) that John

Lester's paying customers have access to delivered to them on a daily basis at the rate of 3 eTraining web pages per day. Study your following 1997 email to learn more about your MLM Screen Pass (and don't expect all of the links in this roughly 21+ year old email to still be working today):

Training March 5th!

From: "John Lester aka the GEMSMAKER!" <nicers@theone.net>
To: gemstars-r-nicers@discussion-lists.com
   Date sent: Fri, 23 May 1997 23:35:54 +0000

Subject: gemSTARS-R-NICErs: (Fwd) Web Page counter & sales secrets of the AGES! Send reply to: gemstars-r-nicers@discussion-lists.com
   To send mail to list, use gemSTARS-R-NICErs@discussion-lists.com

To send mail to DIGEST list, use gemSTARS-R-NICErs-digest@discussion-lists.com

To change your email address, first remove the old one, then request that the new one be added at: lists-admin@discussion-lists.com To be removed email: gemSTARS-R-NICErs-request@discussion-lists.com with UNSUBSCRIBE in the body of your email. If you can't handle the enormous flow of email on this very active list, email: lists-admin@discussion-lists.com to be put on the LIST DIGEST & only receive 1 composite email per day!

WE HAVE A ZERO TOLERANCE POLICY REGARDING VIOLA-

TIONS OF THIS DISCUSSION LIST'S RULES! YOU WILL BE REMOVED IF YOU VIOLATE THEM! READ THE LIST'S 4 RULES IN THE FOOTER BELOW!

Jerry wrote:<g>

————- Forwarded Message Follows ————-

To: gemSTARS-R-NICErs@discussion-lists.com

From: Jerry <globalfn@mako.com> Subject: Web Page counter Date: Sat, 24 May 97 02:43:29 -0700 (PDT)

Hi to the group. I have been reading the list for a while, but this is my

first post. Does anyone know if we can get a hit counter for the Web Page?

It would be good to know how much activity our pitch letter is generating. I just finished a small test mailing, & got a WHOPPING 18.7% response, but I don't know how
    many hits my web page had. Any ideas? Last dumb question How long after the pitch letter (directing them to the BEAUTIFUL Web Page) do you send a
    follow-up & with what? Thanks for all of your GREAT tips,

I really have learned a lot in the short time that I have been reading them.

Have a Great Weekend:-o)) Jerry Snyder

»>Jerry, the hit counter is one of the next things on our agenda. Can't say exactly when it will be here, but it is coming. Thanks for the compliment on the Web page. You have good taste.<g>

Regarding what to do after you send the approved teaser, you then either manually, or through an autoresponder, send the approved pitch. You can get a copy of the approved teaser and pitch at your self-replicating web page at

http://www.nicers.com/YOURADDRESS

whatever YOURADDRESS happens to be. or at http://www.nicers.com the root page.

Here's how I recommend that you followup:

in a day or so, send them an email that goes something like this, and you can use NICErsPRO to do this by simply creating another database like hotleads.mdb or something like that, and remember to use personalization:

Hi ProspectName,

the other day I sent you an email and I haven't heard back from you. I'm an entrepreneur and I am always looking for good business opportunities. Let me know if you know of any good ones, okay?

Sincerely,

Your Name

Now, what you have done here, if you are marketing to network marketers, is put a red cape over your chest in front of a raging bull.<g>

I GUARANTEE YOU that you are going to get a heck of alot of people emailing you back! Since we get paid for TALKING TO PEOPLE, the quickest, fastest and most effective way to get people TALKING TO YOU is to express an interest in what they are marketing. You have two approaches in following up, a wrong approach, and a right approach.

If you come off sounding like a salesperson (wrong approach), then you lose. If you come off sounding like someone who is going to HELP THEM FIGHT THEIR WAR, then you will win the highest percentage of the time that you could possibly win. Which is the best that you could possibly do, which is what you want.

Why is that? Why is this approach the best way to get people TALKING TO YOU?

Well, think of the following picture that hangs in sales offices across the nation:

BACKGROUND: medieval war, soldiers on two opposing sides fighting on horses, using swords, bows and arrrows, and other primitive weapons

FOREGROUND: tent, with a salesperson on one side, arms crossed, legs crossed, looking very cocky and confident, standing next to a machine gun; on the other side of the tent is a General whose gazed is fixed on the war proceeding on the battlefield, and a Junior Officer trying to get the General's attention by stating, "General, there is a salesperson here to see you!" The General cannot see the salesperson because the salesperson is out of sight on the other side of the tent, and besides, his gaze is fixed on the battlefield, and he replies to the Junior Officer, irritably, "I don't have any time to see a SALESPERSON! Can't you see that I am fighting a WAR here!"

Most of you fail in your marketing efforts because your MESSAGE (the Junior Officer), is WRONG!

You broadcast, in so many ways, that YOU are TRYING to SELL SOMETHING to the other network marketer.

Guess what?!

The OTHER NETWORK MARKETER doesn't want to buy your stuff!

Why?

Because she/he is SO CONSUMED, SO DISTRACTED,

STRUGGLING

trying to WIN THEIR WAR, that if you approach them sounding like a SALESPERSON, they are not going to remove their eyes from their BATTLEFIELD and they will

NEVER

even SEE your MACHINE GUN (NICErsPRO, etc)!

Now, wouldn't things have been different IF, INSTEAD of telling the Junior Office that a SALESPERSON was here to see the General, if that salesperson told the Junior Officer (the messenger), that there was a person to see the General that had a piece of war equipment that would VANQUISH the entire army of the enemy in mere seconds?

Do you think that MESSAGE would have GOT THE GENERAL'S ATTENTION?!

You bet it would. The POWER OF WORDS can never be underes-timated in the world of sales/marketing.

LITTLE THINGS make ALL THE DIFFERENCE IN THE WORLD.

So, if you use the sample followup letter above, INSTEAD of asking, have you downloaded the demo (that's what a salesper-son would say), are you ready to buy NICErsPRO (that's what a salesperson would SAY at THIS POINT, TOO early), you are

INSTEAD

sounding like you are interested in helping this person FIGHT THEIR WAR! In fact, you sound like you might possibly be interested in getting on his or her side (who knows, you might WANT to do that)!

So, by using that type of followup letter, you are going to be like putting a RED CAPE over your chest and these other network marketers are going to come CHARGING at you like an enraged bull, wanting to tell you about their products and services.

This is where the SCREEN PASS comes into play. What is the SCREEN PASS? Well, in

FOOTBALL,

the screen pass is where the Offensive Lineman block the rushing Defensive Lineman, but not at 100%, but not so weakly and ineffectively that they tip off the Defensive Lineman into realizing that a SCREEN PASS is underway. What the Offensive Lineman WANTS to have happen is to let that Defensive Lineman get JUST CLOSE ENOUGH to the quarterback so that the RUN-NING BACK is open out in the flat (behind the line of scrimmage to the left or right of the quarterback) with NO DEFENSIVE LINEMEN AROUND (because they are near the quarterback now) and so that the quarterback can just throw the ball over the Defensive Linemen's heads into the hands of the running back so that the running back can take off with alot of open field running room (cause the Defensive Lineman have been drawn to the Quarterback).

The SCREEN PASS in online marketing is where you start asking questions about your prospect's network marketing business.

First off, you might end up actually interested. You won't know unless you ask the questions. However, your primary goal is to LEARN more about your prospect's business and more about your prospect himself. You'll be shocked at HOW MUCH your prospects will tell you about their businesses and oftentimes, much, much more, even personal things, after you show a sincere interest in them and their business as demonstrated by the fact that you are ASKING QUESTIONS and learning about them and giving them an opportunity to tell you about their business, their opportunity, and their products and services.

Now, once they have told you lotsa of stuff about their business and about themselves personally (frustrations, failures, hopes, aspirations, successes, etc), NOW, you are ARMED (or should be) with knowing what their NEEDS are and if you know what their NEEDS are and what their WANTS are, then you know what their HOT BUTTONS are!

Here's where, in an emotionally-charged way, you STRESS to them what the BENEFITS of the NICErsPRO SYSTEMS, and what direct emailing in general, can and WILL do for their business!

So...once you know that they want A (more time with their family, more money, more prestige, more control over their career, whatever it is), you then tell them, in an emotionally charged way, that if they do

A (get their order in with their payment),

34

then you will do B, C and D, etc, (help them personally with NICErsPRO and the NICErsPRO SYSTEMS, offer them the NICErsPRO backup live phone tech support, a Global Email Discussion List chock-full of experienced folks in over 20 countries all over the world ready to assist them and help them learn the globalmobilebiz business in an accelerated group environment, bi-weekly teleconference Virtual Training Meetings, bi-weekly teleconference calls, and much much more), and

HELP THEM WIN THEIR WAR! of recruitment, of MORE ORDERS, etc, for

WHATEVER IT IS that they market!

CLOSE: LET'S GET STARTED! LET'S GET GOING! C'MON, YOU CAN DO IT, OTHERS ARE BEING SUCCESSFUL RIGHT NOW IN THE NICErsPRO SYSTEMS, YOU'RE GONNA BE THE NEXT ONE, AND I'LL BE RIGHT HERE TO HELP YOU! LET'S GO!GO! GO! GO! GO! GO! GO! GO! GO! GO! GO! GO! GO! GO! GO! GO!

10

Conclusion: Your Recommended TOOLS And TIPS

So all of the above is a BIG HUNK of what your MLM Screen Pass Tactic is all about here, Friend. Just like an American football screen pass is designed to get overzealous defensive lineman to over aggressively rush the quarterback, your MLM Screen Pass Tactic is designed to get overzealous MLMers to over aggressively rush YOU!

But there's more.

See, when you're marketing by email, you get people talking to YOU, emailing YOU back by sending out the email letter copy found above in your 1997 email starting in Chapter 8 that indicates that you're an entrepreneur too and always open to learning more about home-based business opportunities.

But if you think that you start pitching YOUR mlm to them the second that they email you back; WRONG!

Remember, when I set up the investment-only appointments with my prospects when I was a life insurance agent, I kept my word and only talked about investments. That's how you earn TRUST! The worst thing that you could do is send out an email telling other people that you want to learn about their opportunities and then immediately start pitching your MLM the second that they write you back via email. That's "bait and switch" and it really rubs people the wrong way. It probably rubs you the wrong way too when somebody does that to you, doesn't it?! See.

But if you're not going to immediately try to sell them your MLM when they email you back, what is it that you're going to sell to them? I mean, after all, you've got to sell them something in order to make some money, right? Even John Carson Lester Jr the 1980s life insurance agent was selling those investment accounts and making some up front money on his way to later selling them the big ticket big commission life insurance WHEN THE TIME WAS RIGHT.

Answer: here's what you sell them. You sell them a TOOL that will help them build the business that they just told you they were so excited about right now (remember, they're on their latest MLM honeymoon). And guess what? Instead of them hating you (for life) for trying to steal their new MLM "bride" away from them like when you used to (before you learned about your MLM Screen Pass Tactic) try to cram YOUR MLM company down their unwilling throats, they will INSTEAD love you for life! Especially if it's a good or great TOOL!

Now, what TOOL does John Carson Lester Jr recommend that

you use? Answer: a LEADS tool. Why is that? Because getting targeted leads that can be converted into productive duplicating recruits in one's downline is BY FAR the #1 crying need of ALL MLMers! Does John Carson Lester Jr recommend that you use LEADS as your TOOL because he is a Leads Company Owner (via MyForbiddenLeads.com)?! No! John Lester recommends that you use LEADS as your TOOL because it WORKS! And how does John Carson Lester Jr know that it works? Because John Carson Lester Jr started using LEADS as his TOOL when he first began running his MLM Screen Pass plays using the AdNet MLM leads company from 1992 to 1995 and then the ProSTEP MLM leads company from 1995 to 2003 and then his personally-owned MyForbiddenLeads.com MLM leads company starting in May of 2003 (AdNet and ProSTEP eventually went out of business which is why John Carson Lester Jr owns his own MyForbiddenLeads.com MLM leads company today)!

Now, when you are prospecting over the telephone using a service like PhoneBurner.com (or many lesser priced alternatives), what do you do? If you're making a live manual telephone call to your prospect or doing autodialer calls to live answer prospects, pitch yourself as being a marketing consultant to the entire MLM industry who helps other MLMers build their downlines! If you're making calls via an autodialer and only leaving answering machine deposits (where they think you made the call personally), casually indicate that you heard about their new MLM business (all MLMers are advertising their MLM business in some way, shape or form if by nothing else talking to their friends and family about it) and wanted to get some more information about it and leave your callback telephone number.

If you're prospecting via postcards, what do you do? Design a postcard that either says that a) you're a marketing consultant to the entire MLM industry who helps other MLMers build their downlines (and include your website addresses and contact information as one would usually do); and/or b) you're looking to do joint-partnerships with other MLMers so please contact me and tell me about your home-based business opportunity (you are looking to do joint-partnerships because at the very least you want to enroll them in to your MLM leads company to help them build their downlines quicker, faster and better—and that definitely is a partnership arrangement)!

Now, at this point, Friend, you may be wondering, but what about my MLM opportunity! When do I get to pitch my MLM opportunity?! Patience, my Friend. Patience. Remember, the meek (who are patient) inherit the earth (according to the Good Book)!

The answer to the question regarding "when do I get to pitch my MLM opportunity" is found above where I describe when and how I pitched life insurance to my prospects I initially pitched the investments to way back in the 1980s when I launched my life insurance selling career. What were the principles that we learned above? We learned to 1) never "bait and switch" by prospecting for investments and then immediately trying to sell life insurance as that will create an enemy for life (likewise you should never "bait and switch" by prospecting for leads and then immediately trying to sell your MLM as that will also create an enemy for life); 2) let the topic of life insurance come up naturally in the following days, weeks and months and, whenever possible, let them bring it up, since most of the time they will eventually (likewise you should never bring up the topic of your MLM but you should rather let them bring it up in the following days, weeks and months, since most of the time they will eventually).

In fact, a repeat of a pertinent passage from above is in order here. Remember this paragraph from above(?):

But far more important than the 73 cents, as I knew from years of previous entrepreneurial experience, was the value of having obtained yet another TRUSTING CUSTOMER. And, as time went on over the next few weeks and months, what do you think happened? Those trusting customers started asking ME about life insurance! And so what do you think I did! I SOLD it to them (actually, they BOUGHT IT from me)! And so I began to "take their temperature" from just talking to them and asking questions whereby I developed a sixth sense and a feel and learned the "signs and the signals" that indicated to me when it was the RIGHT TIME later in the RELATIONSHIP to talk about life insurance.

Now, Friend, you may ask, "how can I be confident that most of the time they will eventually bring up the topic of my MLM if they are so in love with their MLM?!" Your answer is very simple, my Friend. People's emotions can change in mere seconds. You're aware of that fact, are you not? And if people's emotions can change in mere seconds, aren't they likely to dramatically change over the course of multiple days, weeks and months? You bet your bottom dollar they are! Fact is, for 90% of the MLMers who are on their latest MLM "honeymoon" today, most are just several short days, weeks or months (average is about 3 months when you average in those that give up really fast in just a few short days or weeks versus those that hang in there a little longer beyond 3 months to 6 months and sometimes a little longer) from filing their latest set of MLM divorce papers! That's because most MLMers lose money hand over fist because they commit almost every unpardonable sin that one can commit in business (purchase your PiedPiperPrinciple 5 hour 50 minute CD/eBook/Paperback for your absolution)! And if you haven't made them your lifetime enemy by initially trying to cram your MLM down their throat while they were still in their hot and horny MLM honeymoon period, guess who is going to be the guy/gal ready to clean up when they are newly divorced, single and back on the MLM single and looking market again! YOU, the guy/gal that was so helpful and interested in their success right from the very beginning! So, as your RELATIONSHIP with them progresses (as your leads customer), what you then do is to begin to "take their temperature" by asking them questions about "how they're doing in their MLM" and develop that "sixth sense" and "feel" as you learn to recognize the "signs and the signals" that indicate to you that they're about ready to file their latest set of MLM divorce papers and become single, available and out on the MLM market again. Gently probe and then back off several times and pretty soon, before you know it, they'll start asking you questions about your MLM!

You know what comes next!

You're welcome!

Your Coach, John Carson Lester Jr